An Invitation to Pause

An Invitation To Pause

Published by Blue Bungalow Press

ISBN-10:0692490663
ISBN-13:978-0-692-49066-2

Cover photo Mountains at Sunrise
©Stefanus Martanto Setyo Husodo

Cover and Interior Design
by Ellen Klempner-Béguin

Edited by Jeremy Brown

Printed in the United States of America

An Invitation to Pause

musings from a mindfulness teacher

by Janet Archer

For Emma and Jamie
I love you both so much.

Introduction

I have always loved to write, even though I never admitted it, especially to myself. My story was that I didn't think I could write and since I didn't think I could write, I never wrote that much. I stuck to this story for most of my life.

When I was young, I used to spend hours up in the woods behind my house writing stories and plays. I remember running through the back door into the house, yelling for anybody and everybody to come gather around so I could read and act out my latest and greatest. My family always gave me big "oohs" and "aahs" and never discouraged me. This is definitely one of my fondest memories of childhood. Funny, now looking back on this, that there are two things I wish I had saved from my childhood: my stories and my bell bottom blue jeans with all the colorful patches I had sewn on them.

Somewhere along the line I got discouraged and I shut down. I lost my love of writing. Perhaps it happened in school where the emphasis was on where I put the commas or if I had capital letters in the right place. This seemed more important than what I had to say. I started losing my voice and believing that having a voice was not what was important. No one seemed to care, including me at that point.

About three years ago, at the age of 62 I began to write again. I was in a class and everybody in the class was writing articles or blogs for their websites. I declared that I did not know how to write and I also had nothing to say. I wanted people to stop encouraging me; writing and I just didn't go together, much like oil and water.

Then someone offered a suggestion that drastically changed my story about writing.

Don't try to write; start to look.

Now that was interesting and I was listening. I knew how to do that. I had, at that point, been teaching and studying mindfulness, Zen awareness and yoga for years. I was in the practice of looking. And coupling that with what I had recently learned in Life Coach Training — the power that our thoughts have in creating our lives — I was ready for the mission.

I began by really looking as I walked the dogs each day. Not just looking externally, but looking internally as well. What could I see out there, as though for the first time, with new eyes, so to speak? What was going on at the same time inside my mind? How were my eyes and my mind relating to each other? Was what I was seeing externally creating certain thoughts? Were certain thoughts creating what I was seeing? Did my experience change when I was stressed or relaxed? So many questions and so much fun!

I was hooked. Where there had been nothing to write about a few months earlier, now I was back in the woods of my childhood. The world was there for me to play in again. And instead of running in the house with my stories, I began to send them out to people on my email list every other week. The first time I pressed send, my heart was pounding hard and fast. What had I just done? Who did I think I was? Who would care what I was seeing?

But, I cared. For the first time it didn't matter what anyone else thought. I was having fun. I was lit up. Something wanted to be said and it was coming through me, rushing through my body and translating onto the keyboard through the tap of my fingers.

I made a commitment to myself to write 50 stories, to just do it and see what happened. 75 stories later, I'm still writing. There is a voice in my head that still tells me I can't write but I choose not to listen to it. Needless to say, it's gone completely crazy about writing this book.

I started getting responses from my readers about the musings that I had the nerve to send out. Even though I was sending stories of what I was seeing, they understood what I was talking about at a deep level. I was telling them their story, and helping them remember what was and is important to them. Through this invitation to pause, to be compassionate and laugh at ourselves, and to take stock of the precious gifts and moments of this life, my readers felt connected, seen and understood.

If I had stayed stuck in the belief that I wasn't a writer, that I had nothing to say and that nobody cared, I would have withheld my little bit of shine in the world — that one moment when someone may have read what I wrote and it changed the trajectory of their day, week and even beyond. We never know what is possible for ourselves and others when we stay tight and constricted and separate.

So here I am. I have pushed send more times than I can count right now, and I plan to continue for many more. My deepest wish is that you enter this book and find a jewel, something that can guide you, speak to you and help you know that you are not alone, that we are all riding this bus of life together. There are no mistakes. We were meant to meet here, you and I.

And if by chance you have a version inside you of my joy-filled girl from the woods, and he or she has not been let out to venture into the world for some time, I just want to encourage you to set that person free. The world needs what lights you up, now more than ever. It is never too late to push start.

Janet Archer
April 23, 2015

Me at home in New Jersey, 1958.

Contents

The Day Wants to Say Hello

My dog loves to be petted.

Especially when she is on a walk.

She wants to greet and wag for everyone.

A man is rushing down the sidewalk

straight toward us,

doughnut in hand, mouth busy chewing,

reading something that is thrust in his other hand.

He sidesteps my dog.

I say, "My dog wants to say hello."

He looks around,

obviously lost from his reverie of chewing and
reading.

He sees my dog and says,

"Oh sorry, I didn't see you girl."

After petting her, he looks around again

and with a delighted sigh

he says, "Thank you."

The day wants to say hello to you.

I hope you stop

and give her a smile

and a deep, heartfelt

thank you.

Confessions from a Sometimes Mindless Arm Dangler

I have a confession to make.

I'm not always mindful of what I am doing.

I had just finished sending out an email to someone exclaiming that I was going to pay very close attention to everything that I did and make NO MORE MISTAKES BY BEING MINDLESS.

That, at least, was my intention.

Exactly fifteen minutes later, I pulled the handle on a waffle-batter machine at a hotel.

I pulled that handle right off the machine.

Without that handle, the machine began pouring batter steadily out onto the counter, onto the floor, onto everybody standing near by.

After tons of commotion and clean up my eye caught sight of a sign.

The directions

that were posted right there on the machine

saying....Don't pull the handle!

Oh dear, right out of the gate, mindlessness was ahead by one point.

Back at the room, standing fully clothed next to the shower, I leaned over and turned the water on, wanting to allow time for the water to warm up.

Next thing I knew, everything in that bathroom, including my fully clothed self, was soaked. It took me a few more moments to realize that the showerhead had been turned away from the tub and aimed into the room.

I'm not sure where this one falls. I don't normally check showerheads; I usually assume they are pointing in the right direction!

Probably, assuming falls under the heading of mindlessness.

At this point, I decided to take back my exclamation of ALWAYS being mindful.

From now on, I would stop keeping score, do my best to be mindful and leave it at that.

As we drove down the highway, leaving the hotel back in the dust, I decided to embrace myself and the morning's events by practicing the most wonderful healing, free medicine we have in this world: laughter.

I rolled down the window, hung my arm out and watched my dangling 63-year-old arm do some serious wiggle-waggling in the wind.

There was nothing to do but laugh.

So now you know.

I'm not who you MIGHT think I am.

Miss Mindfulness is sometimes a mindless, batter pouring, arm dangler

who's

just plain

happy

to

be

alive,

laughing at herself

every chance she can get.

Me, April 2012

Through the Eyes of Abundance

I pushed start on my little recorder and watched in horror as all the files (recordings) in my folder got deleted.

Instead of number 104 showing on the screen, I was looking at a big old zero.

Zero as in none.

Zero as in gone, all gone, nothing left.

These were recordings I had made for myself of things I wanted to remember.

Recordings of guidance I had received during retreats.

104 pearls of wisdom, nuggets of truth and words of love,

lost in the ethers.

At the exact same moment,

Life,

in its infinite wisdom,

sent a messenger my way.

It flew by, just inches in front of me.

Astounding.

Breathtaking.

The Great Blue Heron.

Swooping in as if it were directing my attention away
from the story and misery of losing the files

and placing it

on the abundance and beauty of life.

Just a turn of the head,

and my view shifted enough so that

where a moment ago lack and loss were brewing,

now there was just awe and joy.

Did I really lose everything as my story told me?

That,

was totally up to me.

I couldn't get back what was gone,

but I could get what was here.

And that was only going to happen

if I was willing

to let go of wanting what I didn't have.

In the end, I chose to ride on the wings of
the Great Blue Heron

and see life through the eyes of abundance.

From this vantage point

I saw clearly that

anything I thought I needed to remember

was already deeply rooted in the depth of
my soul.

Pizzas, Hot Dogs and Freedom

This tale started when I lived in North Carolina as a young newlywed. Every day, as I would drive home from work, I would pass a waving hot dog. I don't even remember who the hot dog was advertising for. I just knew I had to get out of North Carolina because of this waving dog.

You see, I didn't want to live in a place where there were waving hot dogs with smiling faces. I took it personally, like it meant something about me. I wanted to see myself as a young hippie, a homesteader, someone who would never eat a hot dog let alone live in a place where there was an imitation, Velcro-backed, human-sized dog smiling and waving crazily at me every day.

It made me angry, and every day I would rant about the predicament of living in this fake hot dog land.

Basically, driving myself crazy.

Even though I was calling the hot dog crazy,

I was the crazy one.

Life rolled on, as life does. I moved north and found myself living in a neighborhood. That same voice that told me I wasn't someone who should live near live hot dogs began telling me I wasn't someone who should live in a neighborhood.

Twenty years have passed since moving to that neighborhood.

My neighborhood.

And my neighborhood happens to have a walking, talking, waving piece of pizza living there too. I have passed that pizza for years and paid no attention to it, just glimpsing it out of the corner of my eye, pretending that it wasn't there.

I mean, living in a neighborhood was one thing, but one with a pizza walking around it, that was a little too much over the top.

Yesterday I drove by the pizza and it occurred to me; I wasn't mad that this pizza was walking around my neighborhood. There was no longer any charge there. Somewhere along the line, I had chosen not to make it mean anything about who I was.

We can't control the world around us, but we can control what meaning we are going to put on everything.

In my experience, if there is no negative meaning, there is no problem.

I live near a walking pizza. Yeah? So what?

I live near a walking hot dog. OK, so what?

I live in a neighborhood. So what?

We've all got our variations of pizzas and hot dogs running around our lives. We can't get away from them and we don't need to.

Nothing out there means anything about who we are in here unless we make it so in our minds.

And that, my friends, is freedom.

Sweet, sweet freedom.

Go ahead. Have a taste. You just might really enjoy it.

Jersey Girls

My mom Fran and Clara, California, June 2014

One from Newark and one from Elizabeth.

Living out their final years in a sunny coastal town in Southern California.

Clara is the oldest; has Fran beaten by 21 days.

They both turn 93 in September.

And they couldn't be more different.

Clara plays poker every day to keep her mind sharp.

Fran watches Judge Judy because her mind now has some big gaping holes in it.

Clara is holding out for her five-year gold star.

This is her goal.

She is not going to die until she gets it.

Fran already has two five-year stars.

She doesn't care a hoot about them.

If the pin with the stars wasn't attached to her blue jacket, she wouldn't even know she had it.

Fran is tired and complains that she just wants to go back to her room and sleep.

Clara gives Fran a pep talk, one of many.

"Fran, you don't want to sleep. Stop saying that you want to sleep. We have no time to waste here. We've got to do this!"

Clara doesn't mind that Fran's mind is made of Swiss cheese.

But she does mind that Fran speaks of sleeping
away her last years of life.

I sit between them at the breakfast table,

feeling so much love in my heart

for both their long journeys

and their sweet sisterhood.

We get ready to leave.

Clara says, "OK let's hit it girls," as she hoists herself
up from the table and grabs her walker.

Fran watches her go, comments on what an old lady
she is and announces once again that she is tired
and could just go to sleep.

Tomorrow morning they will go through the same
routine.

And every morning thereafter.

Until one day, one of them won't show up for
breakfast

ever again.

Make no mistake.

Maybe we aren't in walkers and our bodies aren't
failing us,

but one day

we won't make it to breakfast.

We have no time to waste here.

Thank you Clara for your 93-year-old Jersey-girl wisdom.

Today I turned 64.

I'm a born and bred Jersey Girl myself.

I hope when I am 93 that I don't have a Swiss-cheese mind,

but if I do,

I hope to have a friend like Clara by my side.

Calming the Heck
Right Down

Considering the state of my mom's mind these days,

I've decided to build some muscles.

Some big bad brain muscles.

Get the old noggin fired up

with some heavy lifting

and multiple repetitions.

I'm on day 27

of a 60-day workout plan.

I can already feel those new neural pathways

pushing through the old sludge in my brain.

I'm on fire.

My favorite brain game involves trains.

Different colored trains going to their respective
colored stations.

Choo-choo.

Sounds easy, right?

Well, it starts out easy. Cute little red train choo-
chooing to its red station. Then the blue one comes
out of the tunnel and I direct it to the blue station.

Easy, fun.

Only

Why is that cute little red train going into the blue
station instead of the red one?

Why are the trains starting to come out SO FAST that I can't keep up?

Why am I getting so agitated and screaming at the computer screen?

YIKES!!!

Holy Moly, I'm a mess. Tight, angry, totally wound up and what???

Game is over and I WANT TO DO IT AGAIN???

Am I crazy?

Apparently so.

I push start.

I know there is a way to do it.

I'm here to train my brain.

There has got to be a secret and I'm going to figure it out

if I have to keep playing this game over and over and over.

Then it hits me.

I know what is missing.

The only reason I was able to break into the next level is because I uncovered the BIG SECRET:

I just have to CALM DOWN

and stop worrying about the trains that I see going the wrong way, tracks I forgot to switch in all the commotion.

If my attention is on those wayward trains, and lost in the "mistakes" I'm making,

I'm sunk.

Train after train is delivered to the wrong station

because my brain has gone to mush

and my attention is on what could have been,

what's wrong, instead of what's happening right now in this moment.

Backward thinking taking me out of any forward movement,

as in frozen, stuck, glued tight, major mind jam.

Who would have thought that building brain muscles would involve calming down?

The more I relax, the better I do.

The more I relax, the better my brain functions!

WOW!

I can relax my way to believing that what I once thought of as impossible is actually possible?

What if I approached every moment like I was just sitting down to play the train game?

Relaxing my brain...check.

Relaxing my body...check.

Letting go of worry...check.

Life chugs on as it does...

Check, check, choo, choo.

My sister Carolyn in Mexico, April 2006

The Easter Lily Show

We were standing over the buckets of lilies for sale trying to pick the perfect bunch to buy.

We settled on some that had no flowers, just lots of buds with the possibility of great blooming to come.

I took them home, cut the stems, put them in water and waited

and waited

and waited

for them to bloom.

Nothing.

I waited some more, now with an added commentary running in my mind about how we seemed to have picked the worst bunch of lilies. They were never going to bloom. I was sure of it.

Every day I would tend to them, talk sweetly to them and tell them to bloom NOW!

I began inspecting them very carefully for any sign of progress.

I thought of taking them back for a refund.

I was leaving town in a few days and I needed some action, FAST.

Something had to be done.

I was annoying myself.

So I decided to change my tactic.

Instead of being mad that they were not blooming,
I decided to admire them just the way they were.

I cooed over them and enjoyed those green buds.

I no longer had any expectation of these lilies ever
blooming.

I let them be.

They were on their own unique timeline, not mine.

For the first time, it didn't matter if they bloomed
or not.

I was enjoying the lilies fully, no blossoms,
no scent.

It wasn't until this change of mind that I fully awoke
to my own faulty thinking.

My previous unhappiness was created from
thinking this one thought:

"These flowers should be blooming because I
bought them at the store for Easter and they should
not be selling flowers that were not ready to bloom
at Easter."

Really, the store can do whatever it wants to do,
as could I.

Enjoy what I had, or not.

The lilies weren't wrong.

My thinking was wrong.

The lilies were just doing their own dance of life

while my mind was screaming, "There is something wrong, this needs to be fixed."

One week to the day of buying the lilies, the first blossom arrived.

It happened as I was rushing out the door to catch a plane.

I was elated to have caught the very beginning of what I have heard was

the most amazing show of blossoms and smells that have ever befallen our home.

Even though I am not there for this amazing show of glory, I love these lilies for reminding me

to be patient,

to be present as an observer of life unfolding,

and get out of my own way when

I try to control

the world around me, which is completely out of my control.

If you are needing a jolt of joy today,

go out and get yourself some flowers

but please remember this:

you are the one in charge

of whether you

enjoy the show.

Bad Mood Rising

I was told once that it is OK to be in a bad mood, just don't pretend it's not a choice.

"Why would I choose to be in a bad mood?" was my first response.

I, like many of you, thought that a bad mood had nothing to do with me, it was simply something that happened to me because of her or him or them or it.

So, I decided to check it out, and the perfect opportunity arose the very next day.

I was sitting outside in my beach chair down at the lake with my dogs.

The sun was shining.

The water was rippling in the wind.

It was a beautiful day by all accounts.

But did I mention the temperature? Or how I was dressed?

I was totally bundled up.

It was 35 degrees and the wind was whipping cold.

Agitation started arising and I began to pay close attention.

I realized that there was a conversation going on in my head that went something like this:

"I want it to be warmer. I want summer back again. I'm not ready for winter. This isn't fair."

I was heading down the path to a BIG OLD BAD MOOD.

I saw it coming and felt it from within, almost like a train wreck about to happen.

And at that moment, I told myself the truth.

I chose to live here.

Nobody forced me to live in a region where summers don't last until December.

This had been my choice and was still what I was choosing; otherwise I would have chosen something else by now.

The truth actually calmed me down and I settled in to the cold, the sun and the view.

Right about then, the dogs began barking.

Agitation started arising again and I began to pay close attention.

The conversation in my head this time was about the dogs.

I didn't want them to bark. I wanted it to be quiet and serene, now that I was settled in with the cold. I didn't want another dog coming around and them going all crazy.

BAD MOOD ARISING. Train wreck on its way.

Wanting to argue with reality does it every time.

So I told myself the truth.

I chose to have these dogs. Less than an hour ago, I chose to bring these dogs to the beach with me.

If someone came along and said, "Hey, I'll take your

dogs from you FOREVER so you can have peace whenever you want," I would chase them away. I don't want anyone taking my dogs from me.

And so it went for the rest of the afternoon.

And so it goes for most of our days.

Our minds are always drawn to what is lacking and what could/should be different.

Playing the choice game is amazingly powerful and extremely calming.

When we acknowledge what we have chosen and take responsibility for it, it feels SO MUCH better than falling down into victim land.

Because, when I take responsibility, I know that I alone am the one who can pull myself out of that bad mood anytime I'm ready to make a new choice.

So, what are you pretending that you are not choosing?

Take a compassionate look inside that crazy mind of yours.

And then,

When you are ready,

Tell yourself the truth.

The truth does set you free.

Every, single, time.

Just Stop

I fell in love with a STOP sign today.

It actually wasn't the physical sign itself that I fell in love with, although up close it had all these cool diamond patterns. No it was more about the meaning that I was giving to those four letters: S-T-O-P.

STOP

Just STOP

Just STOP what?

If I was going to stop something, what is it that I would want to STOP?

Well let's see:

Complaining and whining

Eating too much

Saying I don't know what I want when I do

Being impatient

Gossiping

Procrastinating

Worrying

Being afraid

Wishing things were different than they are.

That's an impressive list.

So,

I could make the choice to STOP.

I really do believe that life would be great without all that worrying and complaining.

But what if I didn't?

What if I forgot to make that choice or I just wasn't able to stop when I was hoping I would?

Well then,

I think I'd be up against the mother of all STOPs on that one.

The question would then be, could I STOP beating myself up for not STOPPING?

Yup, that's the big one all right.

Just STOP the abuse right then and there.

Choose kindness no matter what.

If I STOP or don't STOP, I'm still worth loving.

I like that,

A STOP sign bringing me around to love.

Now that's worth STOPPING for.

My daughter Jamie and Mazzy, July 2013

Woman of the Sea

She totally caught my eye as I was walking down the street in Nantucket last spring,

her steely gaze peering right into my soul.

I backed up to take a closer look, even though it was raining. I was fascinated.

What was her story?

Had she sailed on the front of an old ship?

What had she seen and experienced out at sea?

Where was the ship now and why had she been saved?

Figureheads were said to have been made as a way of warding off bad luck.

Forget the luck.

I think it was all about strength.

Whoever made her knew about the amazing strength of a woman.

A woman who can both give and sustain life.

I think that is why she was put on the front of a ship.

Even without arms, she radiates and beams from her heart,

welcoming and fiercely protecting all at the same time.

Yes, this woman looked like she had been through a lot.

She was tarnished, dirty and perhaps worn out, yet her gaze remained focused and clear.

I believe there was no knocking this woman down.

The ship may be gone, but she remained, her strength intact.

I project she experienced the sea raging against her countless times but she also trusted that the sun would shine once again after each and every battle and storm.

In my life, I am well aware of the times when I am this woman on the prow of the ship, open, willing and unstoppable.

Then there are those other times when all I want to do is hide below deck and hope that nothing will be expected of me in any way and someone else will take care of everything for me.

But this lady asks me to find my strength and join her at the prow of the ship no matter what.

Through any storm that may be raging.

Through any war that may be looming.

She beckons me to follow her.

Into the unknown.

Into the wildness and fullness of life.

She challenges me to stand tall on the edge where the sea and the sky meet, where the horizon goes on and on forever, and move fully forward;

totally exposed,

radiantly blossoming.

My very own

ship of life,

journeying

through

the clear

blue sea.

This is It

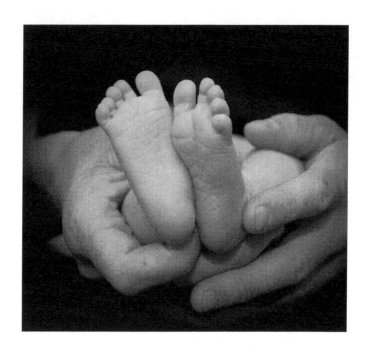

It just takes one moment for your whole world to change.

One moment and everything is different.

Someone dies, someone is born.

Someone walks out, someone walks in.

You're told something that will alter your life.

You decide something that will change your life.

Something happens that affects your body, your mind, or both.

Whatever it is, it is always happening in the moment.

That is really all we have, a string of moments, that when strung together, become our lives.

I am on retreat at a yoga and health center with my husband for a week's vacation.

Ideally, I wanted to relax, move my body in some awesome yoga classes, take lots of whirlpool baths, eat great food and be outside for long walks.

That was my usual experience on retreat, but this time my experience was totally different because of a moment in time when everything shifted.

I was in an afternoon Yoga class when a fire alarm went off about 10 minutes into the class. I had been coming here for 30 years and this had never happened before (to me). Already my mind was kicking into discontent mode. I didn't want a fire drill, and I also didn't want my personal things burning up. We all had to leave the class, in fact, leave the whole building. I was probably complaining about the inconvenience of the fire drill, the long wait, missing the yoga class and the fear of losing my computer in the fire, when the moment of change happened.

I slipped and fell. It was one of those slow dives, where time seems to stand still. As I was falling, I was feeling the pain physically but also the pain emotionally of not wanting this particular thing to be happening to me.

"No, not this, I don't want this. Please can we have a re-do? Can you take this away? Can we start a new scene, one where I don't fall and hurt myself?"

That's what happens; we want to turn back the clock. Oh, if I could have turned back the clock or if I had been more aware in that moment that life was about to shift in the next moment, I would have been so thankful for all that I did have. Walking was easy for me, my body was flexible, I had enough money to even have a computer and be in this fabulous place having a relaxing vacation. I WAS ALIVE, breathing, safe and sound. I was wasting so many moments on complaining, and if those moments make up my life, why wasn't I treating those moments more reverently? How does forgetting what is important happen so easily, only to be seen so clearly on the other side along with all of the would haves, should haves and could haves?

My stay here changed. I couldn't do most of the classes I would have normally done. I couldn't go down to the whirlpool. I couldn't go out for those long walks, but I could take care of myself, eat well, rest, restore and practice being in the moments of my life as it was, not as I wished it was.

We are all affected by the truth that everything happens in a moment, that each moment is all we have.

If this were your last moment on earth or if you really got that your next moment could be one of change, well then, how would you like to be living in this moment? What is most important to you right now?

Look around:

Drink in this life, your life,

The only life you have,

Right here

Right now.

This is your moment, don't miss it.

My mom in New Hampshire, Sept 2005

Three Wild Seniors
out on the Loose

I have a standing Saturday-morning routine teaching aerobics and Yoga. If I don't meet friends or my daughter for coffee afterwards, then I listen to "Wait Wait... Don't Tell Me!" on Public Radio as I drive home. That show makes me laugh my head off.

On this particular Saturday morning, I got "glitzed" up for the dance class, but since it was winter in New Hampshire, that glitzed up top was hidden under a big, bulky winter coat as I drove up to the drive-in for a latte on my way home.

So, I want you to get the full picture. I've got the glitzed up top on, laughing my head off listening to the radio when I pull up to the window to get my order. The woman takes a long look at me, hangs her head out the window and asks me softly, almost in a whisper, "Are you a senior citizen?"

A WHAT??

I mean, I'm feeling really young, carefree and energetic. I've got the top on. Seriously, it's under there.

Senior citizen was not quite what I was feeling at that moment. Nothing was computing in my head. I believe a stunned silence followed while my mouth hung open.

I then heard myself ask in that same soft whisper that she was using. "Just how old do you have to be to be considered a senior?

"62," she replied.

She got me. I fit the bill.

As I drove away I could not stop laughing. What just happened back there kept running through my brain.

Did her asking me that question mean...

That my whole day was now shot because she reminded me that I am officially a senior citizen?

I couldn't still feel young? I now needed to act my age and have an OLDER attitude?

Maybe I should dye my hair so no one asks me if I'm OLD again!

Or perhaps I should be mad at her because she recognized that I looked...well...older. How dare she!

On and on my mind went rambling.

And as it rambled, I sat down and drank that lovely sugar-free decaf latte while I typed out these words on my computer.

And the rambling began to quiet.

I got clearer and saw what I needed to see,

which was this:

The truth is, her asking me that question means whatever I want to make it mean.

Nothing more.

End of story, and the beginning of my own story, which I then can create however I want.

So here it is, as I want to see it.

I am proud of being 62 years old while feeling and acting like I am years younger.

I've got a lot of days under my belt (approximately 22,630) and I don't want to miss this particular one because of worry or anger.

I am so lucky that my body is strong and flexible and that I wear sequined tops that sparkle. I hope I'm still wearing them when I am 92.

She was a really kind woman; I could see it in her eyes. She was happy to give me that 10% discount.

I have so much gratitude for learning that creating a life I love is always only a thought away.

Young, old; my dogs don't give a hoot what I am. As I have been writing this, they have been pacing back and forth in their 12-year-old bodies, anxious for me to finish and get my butt up off the chair so I can take them out for a long afternoon walk.

As the three of us run out the door and down the steps, without a care at all about our age, I'm reminded of a sign I once saw:

Wild seniors out on the loose.

Yes we are.

Life doesn't get

much better

than this.

Tree Face

Have you walked by something many times and then one day you actually SEE what you have been walking by? I mean really see it. Not see what your mind tells you is there, but have a firsthand experience of seeing directly.

That was exactly what happened to me in the woods last fall. Every day I would pass this tree with a face on it. I would comment to myself that it was strange for a tree to have a face on it, but the thing that really got a long conversation going on in my head was that there were no lips.

Why did someone go to all the trouble to put eyes and a nose on a tree and leave the lips out?

I could hear the same repeating thought going on in my mind every time I passed the tree,

That tree face should have lips.

I was no longer really looking at the tree. I was too busy having a conversation in my head. I was sure that I already knew what was on that tree. I'd already seen it hundreds of times, hadn't I?

At some point, I believe, we stop seeing things directly and we just start hearing the experience of what we are looking at through our conditioned mind. We stop looking because we believe we already know it all.

Maybe it was the slanting of the sun on this particular day, or a sound that caused me to glance at the tree from a different angle. Whatever the reason, my seeing and being in the present moment matched up exactly so that my mind was short circuited; there was no thinking, just silence and direct observation.

And there they were.

The lips.

I was frozen in disbelief.

How in the world had I never seen those lips before?

I was so busy believing my story that I never really saw what was right in front of me.

There is a whole new world out there when you begin to really see things through your eyes directly, not through your brains interpretation.

Try it.

Stop every so often today and just look at what is in front of you.

Don't think about it.

See it.

Drink it in.

You will be amazed

at what is there

when you

begin to see things

As though

For the very

First time.

It Feels like Home

I don't know if it was the words coming out of her
mouth or the extreme redness of her face as she
spoke those words to me,

probably both,

but I felt the impact deep inside.

If I could have, I would have willed myself to shrink
into a tiny ball and roll away.

"You were snoring like a drunken sailor last night!"

It was morning.

I was attending a workshop at a place I love,
sleeping in a dorm with a group of other women.

I woke up feeling great.

Apparently, she did not!

Fast-forward a few years to last week.

To beat the snow storm the day before
Thanksgiving,

my husband and I grabbed my 93-year-old mom
and headed out the night before

on our planned trip to New Jersey.

We arrived at our destination late at night
and got a room with two queen beds,

one for my mom and one for us.

I mean, how bad could it be?

It was one in the morning;

we were all tired.

Put my ear plugs in, closed my eyes,

Sweet dreams...

Tick..tick..tick

ZZZZZZZZZZZZZZZ!!!!!!

What the heck is that??

Could it be?

My mom was snoring..just..like..a drunken..sailor!

Now mind you, I have never heard a drunken sailor snore, but this was REALLY bad.

I wanted to throw something at her,

shake her,

but I also didn't want to wake her up.

Since she has dementia, I thought she might get a case of double dementia if she was awakened in a strange place in the middle of the night.

That would not have been a pretty scene.

So I lay there

And listened

And listened

And got mad

And thought about my day tomorrow that was already ruined because of her snoring.

And then I remembered the woman with the red face

And I laughed at the irony of the situation.

I rolled over and whispered to my husband,

"Can you hear my mom snoring?"

And he said,

"Yes, she sounds just like you!"

Then he wrapped his arms around me

And as he drifted back off to sleep

I heard him say,

"It feels like home."

With a heart full of gratitude

And a smile on my face

I, too, finally entered the land

Of blessed rest.

Me and my husband Paul, June 2001

Head in the Wall

I wake up at 3:15 and my head is full of what ifs.

What if it is too cold?

What if it doesn't work out?

What if she is unhappy?

What if this is a mistake?

I saw a mural on a brick wall not too long ago.
A man was carrying a briefcase and he had no head.
His head was portrayed as being stuck inside the
brick wall. All you saw was this headless body
holding a briefcase.

I am a woman lying in my bed and just like the man
carrying a briefcase, I also have my head stuck in a
brick wall.

A thick brick wall.

An unmoving, unforgiving brick wall.

And the only way to get my head out of that brick
wall is to retreat back to where I started from
before my head became encased.

This bed,

These covers,

This body,

Right here,

Right now,

Taking a deep breath,

Feeling the weight of the covers,

Dropping my head into the pillow,

Relaxing my face,

Softening my fingers.

Letting the mantra, "It's all OK, just here, just now, just this; all OK" float through my awareness and soothe every cell of my being.

Breath by breath

my head releases out from the grip and tightness of the imaginary wall.

I feel freedom arising in both my body and my mind.

My head will probably end up in that wall again any time my mind wanders off into future worry and fear or travels back to past regrets.

But that is not a problem.

No matter how many times my head crashes into those bricks, I know how to get it back out.

Remember the Hokey Pokey?

Put your head in, put your head out, put your head in and you shake it all about. Do the Hokey Pokey and you turn yourself around, that's what it's all about."

That's what I do as I finally drift back to sleep.

I turn myself around.

There is no future to worry about, there is no past to regret.

There is only now.

And when later becomes now, I will be equipped with all I need to know to handle whatever I need to handle then.

And that, is what it is all about.

The Ride

There is something about listening to silence.

Deep listening.

When the air is so pregnant with stillness that the least little sound sends tingles up and down your spine.

I was sitting on a rock, close to the top of a mountain,

Being astonished and surrounded by an amazing silence. It was broken only by the occasional wind blowing through the pines and rustling the remaining leaves on the trees.

SSS..WISH

Attention captured.

Then it was gone.

Silence again.

No other humans in sight.

No human sounds to be heard.

Bliss.

That is

Until...

It wasn't.

It was getting dark.

I was in the middle of nowhere; no other humans in sight.

I couldn't see the trail markers and the trails were obscured by all the leaves that had fallen to the ground.

I went from happiness to fear in a split second.

Bordering on panic.

Same view, same trees, same wind.

Nothing had changed externally around me.

But my own thoughts?

They were running rampantly in a most toxic direction.

I started gathering myself together,

sending wave after wave of soothing breaths

throughout my whole body.

"Calm, Calm, Calm,

You can do this."

I started feeding my mind

exactly what it needed

in order to get my legs to unglue from their

ridged fear-gripped lock

and lead me down the mountain.

I found the trail.

I was on my way down when I put my hand in my vest pocket and grabbed hold of my fully charged (forgotten) cell phone that I had so brilliantly brought with me just in case I should run into trouble.

Perfect reception.

It was at that moment that I heard my husband calling to me.

You see, I wasn't really out there all alone.

He had taken a steeper trail all the way to the top.

There I was,

phone in hand and husband in sight.

My mind had taken me for a ride

at a dizzying speed

down the wrong side of the street.

It's not a pretty picture

when you give over,

to your fearful story-filled mind,

the keys

to the car!

Some Patience

Bear in her chair, New Hampshire, Sept 2013

It's 35 degrees out this morning.

Grey sky

Wind, steady enough to feel blisteringly cold
on my face.

I've got my dog on the other end of the leash.

She's old, 93 in people years. Same age as my
mother.

She's slow.

I can't make her do anything she doesn't want to do.

She stands outside the door, sniffing the air.

She is tuned into something that I have no idea of.

I feel the air on my face again and want to get this
walk over with so I can get back inside to the
warmth of my house.

My dog is still standing in a trance.

I know from experience that if I pull, push or
tug her,

she will simply sit down in refusal mode.

So I wait.

This afternoon is the day I go to help my mom
take a shower.

She acts just like the dog.

She won't do what she doesn't want to do

and she doesn't want me to tell her what to do.

She's moving through time and space at her own speed, not mine.

When I rush her at all,

I get the sit down.

If I push,

the sit down just gets longer.

She slowly moves

But I need to be careful, because if I pounce,

She's back down

and who knows when she'll get up again.

Walking my dog trains me to be with my mother.

Being with my mother trains me to walk my dog.

I need patience to be with both of them and some days my patience is just plain buried under 10 feet of heavy snow

with no shovel in sight.

What's interesting is: when I change my "poor me" story from, "they are doing something TO me," to "they are doing something FOR me," it's a fresh new way of being with myself and both of them.

What if my dog just wants me to stop and notice the changing sky and feel that snappy air on my face?

Perhaps she's inviting me to take it all in and get out of the rat race in my mind.

"Isn't it nice here in the moment?" she could be suggesting with her soft doggy eyes.

Maybe my mom wishes for me to settle down within myself;

Quit pushing so hard,

Soften around the edges,

Go with the flow, so to speak.

"Why the big rush? Where is the fire?" she might be questioning me with her motherly stare.

Perhaps all along I was never even in charge of anything. Maybe I was on the walk or in the shower to learn something about myself, something that could help me live a happier life.

If so, then I'm the lucky one, because my mom and my dog seem to be endlessly patient with me as they so deliberately teach me all about patience.

And then

I gotta ask;

Just who

Is really taking care of

Who here?

They're Just Words

Me, in the classroom, New Hampshire, 2006

I just got a comment card about a class that I taught last week.

It said, "the class was fun but disorganized and she appears unprepared."

Ouch. That hurt. I took it personally.

My stomach sank and I got sweaty all over in response to my thinking, which went something like this:

Someone doesn't like my class;

They don't like me;

There is something wrong with me.

I became obsessed with trying to figure it all out in my head as I went about the day. Noodling it in all directions.

I wanted to fix this, make it different, wake up again and start the day over without my dire thoughts about this card.

This is the equation I had cooked up:

I'm fun = I'm a good person = I'm pretty perfect = People like me = I win

I'm disorganized/unprepared = I am not a good person = I'm not OK= I lose.

As long as I had good/bad and right/wrong in the equation, I was dealing strictly in the conditioned world of judgment,

Which never, ever feels good.

I went so far as to look up the words disorganized and unprepared:

"someone who doesn't care enough to give energy or effort toward what they are doing."

HMMM. That didn't sound like me when I am involved with something I love.

I can be somewhat ditzy and spacey, confuse my left from my right, laugh at lot, and be crazy spontaneous,

But I always care and I wanted this person to know that.

I had to let go of making it mean it was important, because it wasn't in the end.

What it became was a great opportunity for me to become more intimate with myself by asking these questions:

Can I be okay with the fact that I got a comment card with words describing my behavior that I clearly didn't like?

Can I own that sometimes I am in fact disorganized and unprepared?

Can I let the words disorganized and unprepared remain as words, not making them either right or wrong?

Can I love myself no matter what part of me is showing up, can I say yes to the whole enchilada?

Fun, spacey, right-and-left challenged, disorganized,
ditzy, unprepared, determined, lazy, prepared,
organized, boring, bright, sullen, awesome?

Can I let other people believe what they want to
believe and not make it mean anything about me?

Last time I checked in, thinking the thought "there
is something wrong with me" has never worked to
make me feel good.

I am so lucky that I have the privilege to teach every
day what I most need to learn.

I get to hear it over and over again:

I am enough.

There is nothing wrong with me.

Me, showing up fully myself in each moment
is enough.

What you think of me is not my business

but what I think about myself

and how often I allow myself to show up as
authentically me

turns into a love fest for this being.

Receiving this little card helped me to come
up with a brand new equation,

one that feels pretty darn good.

Show up. Be me. Repeat = I'm enough, there truly
is nothing wrong with me.

Sweet Gratitude

Balasana.

It is a Sanskrit word for the resting or child pose
in yoga. Bala meaning child and asana meaning
posture or seat.

It is a comforting pose, one that soothes and relaxes
your whole body/mind.

I have been dreaming about doing this pose since
I injured my knee.

I dream about having a knee that will bend and
support my weight on the floor.

I dream about a knee that is not torn up inside.

A normal knee.

I watch my students in yoga class as they are releasing
into child pose with sighs of content and I want to
crawl into their bodies and have some for myself.

And it happened this morning. I had some.

I "tested" my knee out to see if I could go into the
shape, with lots of padding and slowly, slowly, I
dropped in as deep as I could and let go.

And I let go, and I let go and the tears just started
to flow because it felt so exquisite.

I had never experienced the depth of the posture as
I did on this morning.

Each slow, tiny increment of release was bliss.
I had to stay so present and move so slow so as not
to injure myself further.

I was there such a short time in clock time and such a long time in bliss time.

It got me thinking.

Why do we forget to experience the exquisite-ness of everything when we are going about our daily life?

Why are we so rarely present to REALLY receive, to let experiences wash over us?

Why do we take so much for granted?

I have done thousands of child poses in my life and never thought much about it. I enjoyed them; they relaxed me and helped connect me to myself but what was so different today?

Maybe I wasn't thinking about where I had just been and where I was going?

There was no rushing, no sense of urgency to get it done. Been there, done that, next...

There was no room for mind wandering.

There was only presence and tenderness.

I remember many years ago being at an aerobics teacher training and meeting a woman who said something so profound to me that I have never forgotten it.

I was worrying aloud about my outfit, my hair, my legs, whether I would be any good as a teacher or not and whether people would like me and want to come to my class.

She looked at me, smiled, and said, "I am just so thankful that I have a healthy body that can move in such a way that I can even dream about using it to teach others about the joy of their bodies."

WOW. In that moment, she knocked me over the head with a gratitude two-by-four.

Gratitude was not really on my radar in those days.

"Of course I have a body that works, that is a given," was my thinking as a cocky 32 year old.

But she touched something in me that day that has never left my awareness.

And that is what was touched this morning in Balasana.

Sweet Gratitude.

One that calls forth a prayer of thankfulness.

Thank you dear body for what you can do.

We all have this choice; be miserable and thirsty or drink the water of gratitude.

Heck, don't just drink it, roll around in it, jump and play in it.

Open your mouth and hands wide and take in what you've got,

Not

What is not.

The Moan and Groan

Vicki Smith, Sunset Beach, North Carolina, 2014

We are practicing something every moment of every day.

Malcolm Gladwell claims that it takes 10,000 hours of dedicated practice to master a specific task and get to a world class status.

The majority of us don't put in those 10,000 hours but there are plenty of us who do what we love to do over and over again for the shear joy of it and along the way keep getting better and better at it.

We don't have to ask these people how they got there, they show us by what they are doing, by how they are practicing.

Every day last summer when we took early morning beach walks with the dogs we noticed a woman on her yoga mat doing Pilates.

I was curious about her and her story. She had an amazingly toned body and was joyously showing up every day to do "her practice" come rain or shine.

One day I enviously exclaimed to my husband, "How old do you think she is? Seriously, she doesn't have an ounce of fat on her body. She's got to be a lot younger than me!"

He told me he thought she was pretty close to my age, in her 60s.

We made a bet. The loser would take the winner to breakfast.

That's when we met Vicki, the woman with a

dedicated practice who loved challenging her body while breathing in the ocean air.

She had a fabulous laugh and a brilliant smile.

But here's the kicker. She was close to my age, she had just turned 60 two months before.

She asked us to join her the next day.

I told my husband that we were in for it. She seemed like a "do or die" kind of gal.

I was right.

She whipped our butts, laughing loudly the whole time.

Seriously,

She had muscles that I didn't know existed. Muscles that could do things I had forgotten could be done.

While her body went from shape to shape, mine just wanted to lay flat on my beach towel and cry.

I was groaning every time she would yell out, "stay with me now!"

But here is the thing.

She has been practicing Pilates every day and I have not.

In this last year alone, she has put in 360 hours more than me practicing Pilates just by showing up one hour each day.

We all get good at what we practice.

I had a chance to complain about my newly sagging muscles, but why do it?

I have not been practicing buffing them up for quite a while now. It would be a waste of my precious time to be mad at myself for not being able to do what I haven't even taken the time to practice.

It's all about choices, either I choose to practice that which I say I want

or I honestly acknowledge what I am practicing instead.

Since I lost the bet, I needed to take my husband to breakfast.

I was exhausted from the "muscle beach" workout.

We went to the local pancake house where we ate lots of pancakes smothered in butter and maple syrup.

I was so full I had to drag myself out of there, moaning all the way.

Thank God for the 10,000 hour rule.

If it is true that I need 10,000 hours to get really good at something

then I was still a long way away from being proficient

at what I had honestly practiced

all morning long;

a big old heap of the

moan and groan.

Circling Back Around

I'm wondering a lot lately.

Shining the light on some new places of observation.

Yesterday, my mother started stomping on some crispy leaves that had fallen from a tree.

With glee she announced that she loved the sound of the leaves crunching under her feet.

For years I was surrounded by young children who loved to do things like crunch leaves under their feet and have snow land on their tongues as it fell from the sky.

What happens to all that life lived between the young and the old?

Where we practice

Impatience,

Distraction,

Worry

And regret,

More than we practice living in moments of joy.

If in the end we go back to being like a child, where do we think we are going all the time we are trying to get somewhere?

Recently, I've been having the crazy idea that if I can control the weather then I can control how my mom feels.

If the weather is good, my mom will be happy; if it is bad, she will be unhappy.

It makes no sense at all.

I can't control the weather and I definitely can't control my mom and how she feels.

As I'm busy worrying about the long winter coming up and how that is going to affect her, she is busy crunching leaves and laughing.

I'm pretty sure that

this winter,

when the snow flies,

she'll have her tongue out

catching the falling snow.

And my hope is that

I'll have let go and relaxed enough

to be right there

with her,

Dropping

Into that

Moment of joy.

Thank God for the young and the old.

They are here to show us the way.

Let us be smart enough

To listen

And learn.

And lucky enough

to circle back around

to where we started,

to that place that can only be found

when we let go of trying to get anywhere

and instead

simply enjoy where we are.

Me and Blaze, New Hampshire, 2012

Waking Up

I opened the window today.

A lot.

Let air and sunshine inside my home.

It feels like forever ago that I last did this.

I feel light, ecstatic and alive.

Who knew that opening a window could bring so much joy to one being.

Yesterday I was in the car with my mom,

the first time she has gotten outside in about two months.

She opened her window

wide,

rolled it all the way down,

and said, "How's that for some fresh air?"

DIVINE

Not only because it felt good, but because my mom was back from her long winter's sleep.

She had a smile on her face.

Life itself was pouring its way back into her.

No wonder the flowers grow and the trees bud

after a long winter of rest.

How can they not

when life is beckoning and calling,

"Wake up, wake up

wherever you are."

Spring is in the air.

The dial is turning yet again,

to this

not then.

To here

not there.

In this moment

the long wait

has vanished

and the truth of the bird-filled spring air

happening around us

is all that is real.

Please don't mind me

as I pull up a chair and settle myself down into
a front-row seat

for the amazingness

unfolding

around me.

My sister Carolyn on Nubanusit Lake, New Hampshire, 2010

Connecting Under the Stars

The Looney Lake Girls, Nov 2012

It happened one winter's night.

I was teaching a yoga class in a studio that was down at the end of a long driveway.

A long, icy driveway.

I called everyone to tell them to park up on the street and follow the path down, which had been sanded.

There were about 12 of us all nestled into the warmth of the studio that cold night. Peace and quiet pervaded the room. It felt so good. "AHHHH."

"VRMMMM, VRMMMM, VRMMMM." What in the world was that annoying sound intruding on our cozy sanctuary?

When the sound became insistent, I casually peeked out the window and saw a car stuck at the bottom of the driveway.

"Oh, brother. Did I forget to call someone? It better be "one of us" out there and not some fool who took a wrong turn down an icy driveway just to get stuck there and annoy the heck out of us, not to mention potentially ruin the whole class!"

My mind had obviously not come to yoga at all.

By this time, everyone else was peering out the window too.

We saw a woman emerge from the car wearing

high heels and tight white pants. Clearly she wasn't coming to yoga.

"Well that is a relief. We don't need to help her. She's not one of us."

We all stood there,

and that is when the magic happened.

As though on cue, all of us, without speaking, went and put on our coats and boots.

There was only one place for us to be: with this woman. Even though our minds may have been shouting no, our hearts were leading us out to help. We left the warmth of the studio and flooded out into the night, much to the joy of the woman who was totally not dressed for winter and had mistakenly made a wrong turn down our icy driveway.

With much strength and sand, we got her up and on her way.

Her happiness while driving away was not to be missed.

There we were, bundled up against the winter cold with a million stars twinkling overhead, all of us feeling so amazingly relaxed and happy, feeling much like we feel when we leave a yoga class.

In reaching out to another we had found more connection within ourselves.

We were warmed through and through, in spite of the cold.

It felt perfect, her coming down the driveway right when she did.

We came expecting our usual yoga class and through our own willingness to surrender to what arose in that moment, we each found a great calming and joy bubbling up inside.

So, arm in arm, we strolled back into the studio.

Maybe, just maybe, someone else would get stuck tonight.

We were ready.

We were there to practice yoga, after all.

All Together Now

*My sister Carolyn, me, my daughters Jamie, and Emma
and friend Karen, May 2015*

I'm very suspicious about the term, "got it all together."

She's got it all together.

He's got it all together.

They've got it all together.

I wish I had it all together.

If only I had it all together.

When I have it all together. . .

They are so lucky that they have it all together.

I'll never have it all together.

What the heck does having it all together mean anyway?

It sounds like we have scattered our parts here and there and we have to go gather them all up again and hope that they find their correct places and look like the perfect picture of us on the jigsaw puzzle box.

And if we have lost a part or it ends up in the wrong place, well then, clearly, we do not have it all together.

It also implies that there is a place that we have to get to, and until we get there, we are just plain old defective, and the only thing we can do while we wait to get it all together is stay stuck, moan and groan and wish things were different. From this vantage point, it is a big old excuse not to involve ourselves fully in life. All of it is simply a story that we don't have to believe.

I'm also suspicious because I think that once we "have it all together," something new will arise in our life that will change our "all together" status and we will be scrambling around to get it all together once again. It becomes a vicious cycle. One minute we have it all together and the next minute we don't.

Why not live today as if we're not missing anything? That we in fact have it all together, because the truth is, we do. Nothing has ever gone missing, nothing is lacking and nothing needs to be fixed.

If we didn't believe that there was something separating us from having it all together, well then, we would act from a place of having it all together.

We would do that thing that we tell ourselves we can do only when we have it all together:

Make that call, sign up for the class, take a walk, wear that certain outfit, be kind to ourselves. The list is endless.

What would you do if you no longer believed that you had to have it all together in the first place before you could even start?

Well...

What

Are

You

Waiting

For?

Bust the "all together" myth wide open and start living the life you want right now.

Live your life with your party hat on and your horn a tooting.

It's just a thought away.

My daughters Jamie, Emma, and sister Carolyn, New Hampshire, May 2015

Zoltar Has Spoken

I was pouring coffee at my favorite breakfast spot when I heard a man's voice with a foreign accent saying:

"I see you over there, yes YOU, come a little closer and let Zoltar tell you what you need to know!"

Now, I've been coming here for years and this is the first time that the machine with the fortuneteller happened to be plugged in when I was there.

All this time I thought he was just for show.

But he spoke and I was instantly drawn to him, because he was speaking to me, just to me....he saw me over there...RIGHT??

I grew up believing that someone else out there knew what I needed to know.

And here he was, Zoltar, with his blue eyes darting right and left and his crystal ball glowing bright red.

How could I resist?

I was only two quarters away from clarity and true knowledge.

Clink, clink; Down the quarters went and the whole machine came alive as Zoltar's mouth started to move.

"You may have heard this but Zoltar is here to tell you that you can believe it; age is simply a matter of mind, if you don't mind then, my friend, it doesn't matter. So go on, be carefree like a little baby, but first give Zoltar more silver coins!!"

Of course I would give him more quarters, what he just said about age was brilliant! Nothing matters when we don't give it any mind. It's our minding about things that screws us up.

Feeling quite carefree at that point I went about the business of gathering more quarters. I was like a little kid, in awe, as he spit out his first FORTUNE card.

Well, I'm pretty lucky because a man with a top hat and a huge money bag will be ringing my doorbell any day now because "unexpected wealth will arrive!" I've sent my husband out to buy us a doorbell that works, since ours never has. I want to make sure that we don't miss that ring-a-ding-ding when it comes!

He also told me to cultivate a red-haired person because "therein lies a great deal of happiness for you." But then there is that dark haired person who is trying to harm me. If I can get them out of my life, then I will be extremely happy as well. I guess I need to pay attention to the color of everyone's hair and let them in or out of my life accordingly. Somehow, they hold the key to my happiness.

That is how I used to believe and behave. Someone or something outside of myself held the key to my happiness. Somewhere the money I wanted would just arrive at my door, I could just sit back and wait... and wait....and wait.

But hold on, now Zoltar is telling me, **"If you dream about the sun you will have a bright future but if**

you focus on despair you will increase your misfortune! If you think you can or you think you can't...you're right!!"

Zoltar. You are a genius!!

It's all about what we think. Always has been.

We have just wanted to take the easy way out and hope for the ring-a-ding-ding or that someone else would move the world for us, and if they didn't then they were the ones who brought us great unhappiness.

My eight days with Zoltar were coming to a close.

My father in-law had just died, which is why we had come to North Carolina.

When death comes knocking we look for answers, we wonder what this life is all about and just what is of most importance anyway.

We want wisdom and Zoltar didn't let me down in that department.

He had saved his very best for our last day together.

"Remember, a day is a fortune and an estate. If you lose a day, you lose life itself. Each new day is like a wave. Once it has passed, it cannot be called back again."

Zoltar has spoken.

May we all listen.

No Matter What

It's really interesting how the mind works.

My mom says that she just wants to die, she's ready.

She fell the other night.

Crawled all the way from her bathroom to her bed

where her lifeline necklace hangs

because she refuses to wear it.

She says it's too heavy

and looks way too ugly to put on.

But she obviously knows where it lives;

on her bed post,

and she knows how to push the button,

which is not an easy feat,

as I tried to do it once

and didn't signal anyone because I hadn't pushed
hard enough.

She's strong.

And in that moment, on the floor, she forgot that
she wanted to die.

Last weekend, in the car, she was complaining that
she hadn't slept at all the night before,

not one wink of sleep

and she was afraid that she might get sick.

She wants to die, but she is afraid she might get sick.

You would think that she would want to get sick so her possibility of dying would be increased.

I don't try to have any of it make sense.

I don't try to have her see the folly of her thinking and acting.

I don't make her wrong.

I don't tell her how it could or should be.

I've been diligently practicing minding my own business.

Because the truth is, I don't know

what should be.

I just know

what is:

my mom wanting to die and wanting to live.

Even though she has dementia,

she's no different from me;

we both want someone

to hear us and love us,

and we long to know that we are not alone.

"I'll be here for you mom,"
no matter which road
you travel down
and no matter how many times
you change your mind.

Free Falling

A guarantee is a formal assurance of a promise that something will definitely happen.

My conditioned mind cries out for guarantees. It doesn't like mysteries or the unknown. It likes the imagined safety that lies within the word DEFINITE.

Following the flow of life, as it unfolds moment by moment with no assurances of a particular outcome?

No, that is way too scary...for it.

I just signed up to do something.

I have some big fear about having signed up.

It could potentially change my life.

I have no guarantee about any of it, yet I jumped right in and said YES.

I bypassed my fearful mind and skipped right to my pulsing heart.

Now my mind wants to draw me back into a debate and is desperately looking for a list of guarantees.

I have none.

Not a single one.

What I do have is Life,

With all its variations

and flavors.

No matter what I do, I can make the choice to enjoy the ride in whatever direction it is going,

for as long and as far as my sweet breath takes me,

fully expecting that Life will hold me dearly no matter what.

Free Falling

deeply into my life

and being awed

that a life not driven by the need for guarantees

is the most vibrant, explosive, riotous

masterpiece I could ever hope to create.

Then and only then will I find what I have always been searching for all along,

that peaceful

soft

landing

within.

The Mountains of Life

These words from a song caught my attention today; "when you get to the top of the mountain and look over..."

It got me thinking. When I have stood on top of any personal mountains of life that I have climbed and looked over the edge, I have seen my own amazing strength, which I usually never think I have, especially when I am standing at the bottom looking up.

I have seen my willingness and am blown away because "I can't" rears its ugly head so often in my mind that I am surprised I was able to lay those words down long enough so that I could walk right over them as I made my way on to something much, much better.

And then there is the expanse of love.

Love as far as the eye can see, love that came from deep within and propelled me forward, arising not just when I thought I was being a "good girl" or doing the "right thing" but also when I veered off in the wrong direction or did something very unskillful and didn't believe I had the right to be loved.

And lastly I saw courage. The courage to even take the journey in the first place, especially when "I can't believe this is happening" had landed on my doorstep once again.

Strength.

Willingness.

Love.

Courage.

I know you know what I mean. I have watched and been amazed at what I have seen people do, real people just like you, sometimes against all odds.

"I don't want this" happens and you still get yourself out of bed, grab your boots and put them on.

You don't feel like you are strong enough and yet you take that next step and then another.

We all have had our own personal little mountains that we felt we might not get up and over.

But somehow we have.

And together, we have been showing the world every day in countless ways that

Anything

Is

Possible.

Me on Pack Monadnock, New Hampshire 2012

In Gratitude

There are so many people who have helped bring this book into the world. My students and clients through out the years, I am sending you all such deep gratitude. Those of you who have been reading my musings, it is because of your encouragement that you are holding this book in your hands right now.

Ferris Buck Urbanowski for being the bright light that started me on this path. Jon Kabat-Zinn and Cheri Huber for showing me the way and Brooke Castillo for reminding me again and again that anything I want is just a thought away.

Jeremy Brown for reading every word I wrote with such loving care and then thanking me for the opportunity to do so.

Ellen Klempner-Béguin, the most amazingly talented designer. I couldn't have done it without you! Creating this book with you was the most fun ever, a joy from start to finish.

My husband Paul, who has always patiently listened to my stories and lovingly supported me when I was bursting at the seams to read them to someone.

My sister Carolyn, who nominated herself President of my fan club and has never tired of the job.

Michele Kittell, queen of words and coach extraordinaire who encouraged me relentlessly to put these words out into the world.

Lastly, to my mother, who inspires a story in me almost every day.

Dear Reader,

I hope you enjoyed reading this book of mindfulness musings. I trust you found many that touched you deeply so that when you finished, put the book down and looked around, you began to see life in a new way. A fresh perspective always opens up our inner and outer world to wonder and joy. It feels like freedom and expansiveness and we want to stay in that feeling forever.

It's usually at that point that we vow to remember the teaching and put it into practice but somewhere along the line we may forget and drop back into old habits, beliefs and thoughts - ones that lead us to think "this isn't for me; it's too hard; I can't do this," and the feelings of freedom and expansiveness begin to slip away.

That's what is so beautiful about the time we live in. Whenever we forget to remember and practice what we most want to remember and practice, we are just moments away from someone who can remind us of what we have forgotten and guide us back onto the path we most want to walk.

I invite you to let me be that for you - your own personal guide. If you are a woman whose parent has dementia, I can help you find that fresh perspective so your relationship with your parent doesn't drain the life right out of you. I can remind you how to stay present with what is, in an open, accepting way when your mind starts wandering back into what you wish still was or looking forward into the fear of what you think will be.

To thank you for reading, I would like to offer you a complimentary 30-minute Mindfulness Exploration session to get you started and focused on your journey. Simply visit www.janetarcher.com to schedule a time to talk. I will personally answer any of your inquiries and discuss your best next step in this great adventure you have embarked upon. It would truly be an honor to work with you. I look forward to hearing from you soon.

With much love,
Janet

Summer, 2015

Photo Credits

To access the audio's online,
please visit the link below:

www.janetarcher.com/aitp-audios

23680410R00084

Made in the USA
Middletown, DE
01 September 2015